HAROLD KLEMP

THE
LANGUAGE
OF SOUL

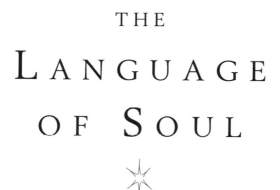

HAROLD KLEMP

ECKANKAR
Minneapolis

ABOUT THIS BOOK: *The Language of Soul* is compiled from Harold Klemp's writings. These selections originally appeared in his books published by Eckankar.

The Language of Soul
Copyright © 2003 ECKANKAR

Printed in U.S.A.

Compiled by John Kulick
Edited by Joan Klemp, Anthony Moore, and
Mary Carroll Moore
Text photo by Robert Huntley

Library of Congress Cataloging-in-Publication Data
Klemp, Harold.
    The language of soul / Harold Klemp.
      p. cm.
    ISBN 1-57043-195-7 (alk. paper)
    1. Meditations. 2. Eckankar (Organization)--Prayer-books and devotions--English. I.
    Title.
BP605.E3K5643 2003
299'.93--dc21

                            2003051186

CONTENTS

Dear Reader

The purpose of this book is to help us remember our divine origin. Our true identity is Soul. Created out of divine love, we exist because of God's love for us—a truth both simple and profound.

Expressed in these pages are truths that will help open the doorway to heaven—seeds to grow our own realization of ourselves as Soul. You are Soul holding eternity in the palm of your hand.

Take one each day and contemplate its meaning. May you gradually come to remember your true identity as Soul, a spiritual being, a true child of God. The keys to a more meaningful life are at your fingertips.

HARMONY

*S*oul, a particle of God, is blessed with the gift of creative imagination, which finds a solution for every problem.

*M*any times the bounties of the Holy Spirit are held back from us because we don't ask. We want something to come into our lives, and we just sit and wait. But if we ask for it, we may just get it.

*E*ven if you are living a nine-to-five life, you can make it an adventure. We owe it to ourselves to live life to its fullest in whatever we do. And the motivation to do this must come from within.

*T*he quest for God is the quest for true happiness.

*W*e are Soul. This life is an opportunity for Soul to get rich experiences in any way that It can—uplifting, constructive experiences, the kind where we find ways to serve all of life.

*T*houghts are things, and it is important to keep our thoughts of a spiritual nature, to put attention on living a life that is a clear step toward growth.

As you grow in spirituality, your whole life must improve.

Sometimes the Holy Spirit may work in a gentle way. It may give you just a nudge, a feeling of how to act, what to do, which dentist to go see—something right down to earth.

*D*ivine Spirit has a way of doing exactly what is right for everyone concerned at the moment.

When you're making a decision about something, look at more than the benefits you'll get by doing it. Also look at what price it requires of you. Weigh *both* the benefits and the price before you decide whether to act or not.

When something appears to go wrong, look for the lesson in it for you instead of finding fault with anyone else or even yourself.

The secret of a balanced life is to live each moment in the right spiritual frame of mind.

*L*earn to give, without ever thinking of a reward. That's how to find the treasures of heaven.

Whenever you're in doubt about any action, ask yourself: Is it true? Is it necessary? Is it kind? You can also ask, What would love do now?

*B*efore you can improve your life and find a measure of happiness, you must learn to do one thing every day out of pure love. That means, don't expect anything in return—neither thanks nor happiness. Pick that occasion carefully. Then, whatever that one act of giving of yourself to someone else is, do it with all your heart.

TRUTH

*E*arth is a classroom that brings about the spiritual maturity of Soul. When Its education is completed, It must decide for Itself what belongs to the realm of timeless truth and what is merely a subterfuge—a shadow of truth.

*T*he window of heaven is what all truth seekers are trying to open.

*W*hen you ask God, "Please show me truth," and you haven't used your talents today, you can't expect to find the greater talents, the greater truth, tomorrow.

*L*ife is a mystery until we come to the path of ECK (Divine Spirit) and begin to understand that we can be the creators of our own world.

*T*he principles of Spirit are embedded in the literature and in the life of our culture. Truth is never hidden. It is always available for the Soul who wants to take the next step.

When you ask for truth and your heart is pure, Divine Spirit will take you one step closer home to God.

*T*ruth is so simple. So why doesn't everybody know it? Because it's too simple. Because we have our preconceived notions about what truth is or what it should be.

*B*y asking, you have reached out and taken the initiative—a first step that will lead you to the next answer.

*U*sually the seeker is not aware of truth within arm's reach, because his limited vision can capture only the hard realities caught within it. There is nothing wrong with this. There is always another step to truth.

$\mathcal{G}$od's love is always working to help Soul find Its way back home.

*N*o matter how much insight we gain about God, there will always be something that lies beyond the horizon of our understanding. That is simply the nature of truth.

*T*ruth brings divine love. The reason for war, theft, lies, and other natural traits of humans is that no religion can drive love into anyone's heart.

When God's love enters the heart, only then can a change for the better occur.

*T*ruth does not operate in a vacuum. People who've been touched by truth try to express it in their daily lives: within their family, business, or religion.

HEALTH & HEALING

*O*ur body is a temple of God. We must take care of it because it is a house for Soul.

*T*his is how we work with Divine Spirit. We try to look at life and find the laughter wherever we can, whenever we can, because laughter is the healer.

*H*ealings always depend on the individual: How conscious is that Soul?

✳

*I*n time of need, help comes if you know how to open yourself—sincerely, without any preconditions or any ideas that God should act in this way and do this or that.

*P*aying attention to foods can help you lead a better spiritual life. People ask me, "What is good food?" There is no good food or bad food for everyone. It depends upon the individual, upon his particular health condition. Who can best tell what's right for you? You can, of course.

*T*he condition of health that we suffer is actually a tool to raise us another degree in our state of consciousness.

Spirit will begin to heal only if you are willing to first help yourself.

When you ask the Holy Spirit for healing, you must open your spiritual eyes and ears to watch for and listen to how the Divine Force is bringing about a change for you.

A healing can happen instantly. Or it may happen in other ways, such as when an individual comes in contact with another person who says, "Hey, here is something which may help you." It's still up to the individual to open his consciousness and accept the different way of doing things.

*S*pirit acts in a way that is for the good of the whole, sometimes bringing a healing of the emotions or the mind instead of the body, because that is in the best interests of that particular Soul's unfoldment.

At times Divine Spirit heals directly, at other times It leads one to the right medical doctor. Sometimes It will assist in the healing and treatment we are presently undergoing. We must inwardly turn everything over to the guidance of this Supreme Force while making every effort to find the most suitable medical help.

*M*ost of our problems are self-made. When things go wrong, if we take responsibility and do something that gives us greater understanding, life becomes easier.

This is how it should be, rather than having someone always giving us spiritual, emotional, or physical healings.

The idea is not to hide from life: It is to live life, but without making the same mistakes we did before.

As Soul, you are like a balloon that rises above the ground. The higher you go, the farther you can see. And the farther you can see, the better you can plan your life.

HELP IN DAILY LIFE

*I*t's quite a discipline when we're in trouble to think of God and say, "I need some help."

*I*f you want to bring yourself closer to the Holy Spirit, say, "I am a vehicle for God and Divine Spirit." Then begin your day with joy. Know that everything is being accomplished as it should be.

*L*ife is a series of interconnected wheels. Very little can happen to you without it being known ahead of time by you. All you have to do is learn to be aware.

*Y*ou are living the spiritual life when you conduct yourself and your business in the name of Divine Spirit. You touch many Souls during the course of the business day. Although you may never say one word openly to your customers, Divine Spirit touches all whom you meet, in some manner or another.

Give your best effort each day, and leave the rest to Spirit.

The way to work with Divine Spirit in our daily decisions is to consider quite honestly: What would I really like to do?

One must put aside thoughts of asceticism, thinking that God loves us more if we are poor. A business decision must be made using all input that's available. What's good for me, my family? It must allow one to grow.

Any decision is not without setbacks, for that's the nature of life. What sets you apart is that you give it your best effort and more, staying open to the subtle nudges of Divine Spirit.

*T*here is usually somewhat of a struggle when we move into a higher state of awareness, and that is natural. The problems in life can be dreaded with fear, or they can be seen as opportunities for growth—and a challenge.

You must make up your own mind as to what you want to do. Consider all parts of your life, the financial and emotional included, and do what seems to be common sense. Then plan and work carefully.

When you don't put a definite shape to what you imagine, Divine Spirit can have unlimited freedom to fill that mold. But if you put a limit to it, you often strike out because you've allowed for only one possible outcome.

*T*he spiritual life is an active one. We recognize that each experience that comes our way is spiritually instructive.

If someone needs our help, we do what we can to the best of our ability.

*M*any feel that a person who spends his time soul-searching is more holy than a merchant who hawks his goods at the market. A highly spiritual person is actually one who has found the comfort zone that exists somewhere between the two extremes.

*I*f we want to keep the blessings of life coming to us, we must learn to be grateful for whatever is given.

CREATIVITY
&
SELF-DISCIPLINE

How does one live the spiritual life? The answer is simply to live creatively, because each of us is working to become a Co-worker with God.

*W*hen the blessings of Spirit are given to us without struggle, we don't recognize the treasure that is in our hands.

*D*ivine love is not something you can talk about, but it is something that you can demonstrate as you live.

A person with a golden heart is filled with love and likes to see something that he starts completed and done well.

*D*ivine Spirit often begins working for our welfare after we have made some small effort first.

The love and protection of Spirit surround you at all times but must be accepted with a loving heart.

*Y*ou cannot measure spirituality by the number of bad habits you have or not. Nor by a certain number of experiences. Awareness of the moment and a joy for living can also be an indication of where you are spiritually.

*S*o few know what a love for living means. They've put a web around themselves and called it spiritual. Life is a celebration. Some will read that as wanton living, but true celebration is loving God and Its own.

*P*eople with a high state of consciousness are not frozen into inaction by terror brought about through disasters. They immediately make a plan to turn the negative energy to advantage. At this level of creative imagination, Soul is in a condition of survival. The lesson of the worlds of matter is to develop Soul's ability to ride the crests of life. This is *vairag*, detached love.

*C*reative people who cherish the gift of life often slip into the secret chambers of the creative mind. Their solutions are well-rounded, more sensible than those of people who rely solely upon reason as their mainstay. Gratitude unseals fountains of creativity, because a grateful person is relaxed. This allows him to take stock of his circumstances with an objective mind. A creative person often gets three-dimensional answers to his problems.

*T*he Holy Spirit will give us all that we need. First we must learn to expect the best in life, and be willing to plan and work for it. Second, we need a clear mental picture of what we desire. Third, this picture is to be maintained constantly, with the certainty that Divine Spirit will supply any rightful desire. Fourth, there must be gratitude for every good thing received.

*E*very problem contains a solution. The key is self-discipline and surrender of the mental habits to the Holy Spirit.

*C*reativity, bountifulness, and gratitude go hand in hand.

*T*he cycle of creative action begins with the concept we carry in our minds of what we wish to do. The next step is to outline on paper some plan of how to accomplish this. The final step is action in carrying out the plan.

LOVE, RELATIONSHIPS, & FAMILY

*O*ne of the biggest lessons we can learn in life is to do everything possible to reach an accord with the individual we are having trouble with.

*A*s we come out of our childhood of spirituality into greater states, we learn to let people be.

*B*efore we love God, we must love all things with the high kind of love, which is called charity. We become the best we can be through the discipline of divine love.

*Y*ou can't make yourself closer to God by hating someone else, whether you believe it's righteous anger or not. The relationship between Soul—which is you—and God is one of love. And where there's pure love, there is no room for anger of any kind.

*T*he Holy Spirit works in subtle ways, but you have to remember to ask. Most people can't hear. You learn how to listen and how to see the messages from the Holy Spirit that come to you—and everyone—every day.

*I*f we realize that our field of dreams is not the same as someone else's field of dreams, we'll get along better with that person. This is a hard thing to learn sometimes.

*T*he marriage bond can only be sacred if it is sacred to the two individuals who have agreed to this union. If they are one in heart, how can they be divided?

A true marriage has commitment by each person. Both realize the responsibility of that commitment. A marriage of the heart lets each of the couple remain an individual, but the two are as one.

*G*od loves Soul rich or poor. God does not necessarily love the poor more. God loves Soul. We can enjoy the things of this life and support our family with material goods with no feelings of guilt.

*H*armony in a family is a sacred thing.

We are required spiritually to act with the greatest degree of responsibility both to ourselves and to others. This is what it means to be part of the community of Spirit, of the ECK—to be part of the cosmic system of life.

*P*eople of the golden heart are full
of love and have the ability to give of themselves. They are the shining lights.

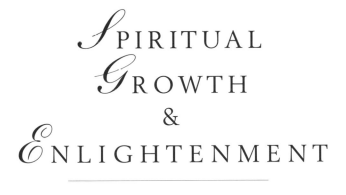

SPIRITUAL GROWTH & ENLIGHTENMENT

*T*he reason for spiritual enlightenment is not to escape life, but to learn how
to live it richly, to enjoy it.

*O*ne of the principles, or laws, of Divine Spirit is that there is always one more step. There is always one more heaven.

A person who has a high degree of spiritual unfoldment will be balanced in his everyday life. He will use common sense and common courtesy with the people around him.

*W*hen greater amounts of divine love come in, we must give out greater service.

*T*he higher you go in awareness, the more you expect of yourself, because Divine Spirit is saying to you, "There is always a better way to do it." It gently nudges you to bring out the best.

*T*he further you go in the spiritual life, the greater becomes the responsibility. And the greater the responsibilities become, the greater becomes the need for self-discipline.

The tests that are easy for us are difficult for others. This is the nature of life. And it means that we, as human beings, must learn patience and compassion. The wheel always turns.

*T*he miracles that happened in the early Christian Church still happen today. To see and benefit from them, all we need to do is open our consciousness through spiritual exercises.

*W*hen you become as little children, you shall see the kingdom of heaven. You will carry no ideas from the past to hold you, none of the future to frighten you, but just the present, with the assurance that everything you need to know is already at hand—every answer, every solution.

A Co-worker with God is some-
one who has learned self-discipline in spiritual things.

As we raise ourselves in the spiritual consciousness, we are better able to solve the problems of life. We are happy. We are at home in every environment.

GOALS, GROWTH, & CHANGE

*B*ecoming a conscious vehicle for God requires that you become the very best you can possibly be, no matter what you choose to do.

*U*nfoldment is a two-step process. First, knowing the way; second, walking it.

*I*f you can achieve an improvement over yesterday, even if it's small, you have gained significantly. You are taking charge of your own world. You are becoming a creator.

*T*he tests of Spirit are unlimited.
They reach you in a totally unique way.

When something goes wrong in your life, there is usually a spiritual reason for it. Divine Spirit is trying to teach you something about truth.

*L*ove tries to find a harmonious way to resolve each situation.

The secret to getting rid of fear is opening the heart.

*O*ur freedom stops where someone else's starts. This line is called responsibility.

*W*hatever you are going through today is training for tomorrow. You need today to reach tomorrow.

*W*hen we give up attachment to everything, including the little self, then we find wisdom, power, and freedom.

*I*f you can dream something, you can do it.

As long as you do not align your actions with your dreams, you are not fulfilling your destiny.

Build. Act in an uplifting manner, and the Law of Life will never repay you in a negative way.

𝒴ou do what you can to make your life right. And when you have done 100 percent of everything you can do, Divine Spirit steps in with the miracle.

$\mathcal{L}$OVE

When we are filled with love, the protection of Divine Spirit comes to help us in our daily lives.

*U*ntil one finds the way to love, to truly love, he will never understand the Spirit of Life.

*N*ot to get attached is often taken to mean "not to get involved." It actually means not to let your idea of how things should be dictate the relationship. That kind of love has strings attached. It means always trying to have your partner do what you think is right.

*T*hose with pure love do all they can to let their mates grow in every way. Detached love means to let others exist without forcing our will upon them. That is spiritual love.

*T*he secret is that one cannot live without love. You've got to find the kind that agrees with your spiritual makeup. Once you have it, you find it a delicate thing that can slip away like water through the fingers.

*M*ercy and compassion are two
very important qualities, but love is the
greatest of all.

*B*egin with the love you have. Love gratefully. This love expands your heart into a greater vessel which can hold yet more love.

On the outside, divine and emotional love may look the same, but divine love is joyful, thankful. It gives itself fully.

Let love be what it will. Don't let the mind tell you one is human and the other divine.

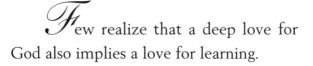

*F*ew realize that a deep love for God also implies a love for learning.

*H*ow do you keep in step with the spiritual laws—and lessen the wear and tear upon yourself? Simply love.

*I*f you make a meal, put love into it instead of the frustrations of your day. Because whatever is put into the food is a reflection of what you have inside yourself, and it goes out to your family, it goes out to your friends. And it makes a very real difference.

*T*ruth becomes more sublime for an individual who develops in himself the capacity to give more compassion and love to all creatures.

*W*hether you are out in the world or you're at home, you are simply an instrument of God's love in your own universe.

SPIRITUAL PROTECTION & SOLVING PROBLEMS

*D*ivine Spirit opens up new opportunities, but we must take them. We must make our own choices with the best information at hand.

*W*e are personally responsible for our own state of consciousness. As Soul unfolds toward total freedom, It understands total responsibility must be accepted for every thought and action.

*T*roubles that come to us are for our purification. They come to us because we must learn a divine law.

*T*he love and protection of the Holy Spirit are with you in all spiritual concerns.

*T*he Holy Spirit often works through professional medical people to help us out when we're in trouble. After all, all healing comes from Divine Spirit, no matter what It chooses as Its instrument.

*I*f you fill your consciousness with
the positive aspects of Divine Spirit, there
is no vacuum where the negative may en-
ter.

*A*s our self-discipline increases, we discover that life can no longer defeat us. We move tranquilly under the protection of that Presence we know as the ECK, or Divine Spirit.

*M*any people do not understand that life, with its burdens, is a treasure. The weight of disappointment makes us close our eyes to the gift of being in the world to learn about the loving heart.

*S*elf-discipline is an absolute necessity if one is to have a productive spiritual life. Replace old tastes and preferences with new, better ones. But do it in the name of the Holy Spirit, with love and a sincere heart, or nothing will come of this experiment.

*N*o two people are alike. Each has an agreement with life that is unlike any other. Learn love, patience, and grace, because they are the way to find harmony.

Finding peace is a big part of your spiritual life.

When you ask for help, Spirit begins to bring changes that are for your good. Of course, this means you must be extra careful in the choices you make. Before Spirit can make any changes, you must develop a better image of yourself: You are Soul. God's love is for you.

THE
GIVING HEART

We must first give to life if we expect life to give anything in return. This is the divine law.

*W*e do all we can to keep the good-will of others as we go about gathering our rich spiritual experiences in this life. But we do recognize limits.

As we give of ourselves, of our patience and love, to someone else who needs it more, something changes inside us. Something flows in, a flow of good feeling. A spiritual upliftment occurs both in us and in the person receiving the love.

*B*ecause of the restrictions of business and running to make appointments, some people don't often feel there is time to be human, to let others know they're appreciated. Other people have an attitude that says, "I like your company. We have to do business and we might as well enjoy doing business."

People who have this attitude are openhearted. They love their work. And through this love for their work, they are reflecting the love of God.

*Y*ou find you get a great deal of love and interest from just looking after the well-being of those Souls who are looking to you for some of their spiritual food.

*S*ometimes you are called upon by the Holy Spirit to go out of your way to help another person toward the enlightenment of God.

*B*ecome an expert in something. You need to be grounded in something. When you do something for God, for the highest principle, you do each step until it sings.

The creative mind of man is imbued with Spirit when it creates anything which is for the good of man.

When we reach the point in our unfoldment where we are treating others with love instead of fear, anger, or vanity, we've made a very important step back home to God.

*S*ometimes it's important to just stop and be grateful for the blessings that you already have.

*O*nce the Holy Spirit grants us Its blessings, how often do we remember to acknowledge them? Acknowledgment is done through gratitude, which keeps our hearts open to love.

*I*t's a pleasure to be around someone who's shining with the Light of God.
People don't always understand what's
going on, or why this person is drawing
them toward him. But there's something
special there.

A gift of true love is always God's love to you that you give to another.

CONSCIOUS LIVING

Happiness is not a matter of how your outer life appears to someone else. Happiness is a state of consciousness.

*V*ery often, we are confronted by people who want us to pray their way or colleagues who want us to think their way. We must remember to maintain our individual relationship with God. We have the shining light of Soul, and because we have it, we also have the wisdom of God.

*P*eople who are able to help in the work of the Holy Spirit are those who are able to help themselves.

*T*hose living the high spiritual life are the knowers, not believers. There is a world of difference between knowing and believing.

*T*oday someone said to another person, "You are so lovely."

And the other person answered, "Because you are seeing yourself."

And of course, it caught the first person by surprise. Generally we see in others what we are ourselves.

When you work with the fullness of heart, the golden heart, you find things are being done right you never realized were being done right. This occurs when there is balance and you have the perception to see the true value of things that come into your life.

*T*he principles of the spiritual life are embodied in everything that we do. If we think they are not there, it is simply because we can't see them or recognize them.

*W*hen you get out of the habit of listening, the voice of Divine Spirit becomes weaker and weaker. Not because It is speaking in a quieter voice, but because you have turned down the volume control on the inner instrument of Soul.

*P*rophecy can come through in the dream state, or it can come through what I call the Golden-tongued Wisdom—where something in your daily life suddenly pops forth. It's as if golden light surrounds it and gives you whatever you need just at that moment.

We must learn to be totally responsible for all our actions, our deeds, and our thoughts.

*W*hatever you do, wherever you walk, walk in the name of Divine Spirit. Walk in the name of God.

About the Author

Author Harold Klemp is known as a pioneer of today's focus on "everyday spirituality." He was raised on a Wisconsin farm and attended divinity school.

In 1981, after years of training, he became the spiritual leader of Eckankar, Religion of the Light and Sound of God. His mission is to help people find their way back to God in this life.

Harold Klemp speaks each year to thousands of seekers at Eckankar seminars. Author of more than forty-five books, he continues to write, including many articles and spiritual-study discourses. Harold Klemp's inspiring and practical approach to spirituality helps thousands of people worldwide find greater freedom, wisdom, and love in their lives.

ALSO BY
HAROLD KLEMP

*Available at bookstores, on-line booksellers,
or directly from:*
Eckankar
P.O. Box 27300 Minneapolis, MN 55427
Tel (952) 380-2200 Fax (952) 380-2299
www.eckankar.org

A selected list:
Autobiography of a Modern Prophet
A Modern Prophet Answers Your Key Questions about Life
The Art of Spiritual Dreaming
How to Survive Spiritually in Our Times
The Spiritual Laws of Life